Poetry from the Bed

Poetry from the Bed

Life with ME/CFS

Oxfordshire Myalgic
Encephalomyelitis Group for Action
(OMEGA)

Published by Oxfordshire Myalgic Encephalomyelitis Group for Action
(OMEGA), 2012
www.oxnet.org.uk/omega

ISBN 978-0-9574170-0-7

Poems 'A Fashionable Disease' by Vivien Steels previously published in
MEMO 1995, and 'So You Have ME' by Vivien Steels previously published in
SMITHS KNOLL 1998, PROMISE 2003, WRITE-AWAY 2003, MESH 2007

The views expressed in the poems are the opinions of the individual poets
and do not reflect the views of OMEGA

Printed and bound in the UK by Lightning Source UK Ltd

Acknowledgements

This book is the work of many people, all doing what they could, within the limitations of ill health or busy lives, including the unseen support of our family, friends and carers. We'd like to say thank-you to you all.

Thank you to all the poets – and to all those who would have loved to have written, or finished, a poem but were too ill. To the poetry competition organisers: Tessa Keys, Pat Williams and Joanna Breheny, who ensured that this book would be full of wonderful poems. To Vivien Steels, who gave up her time to read and judge all the poems and give her valuable feedback. To Matt Trewhella for his help with publicity. To the Poetry Book Group: Jan Seed, Joanna Breheny, Jane, Susie Geddes, Jo and John for their hard work, ideas, optimism and determination. For editing and proofreading help – Pat Williams, Patricia Wells, Sarah MacBean and Susie Geddes. To Lesh for all his back-up support with the practicalities of publishing and distribution.

For the wonderful art work that enriches this book thanks to: Jill Woodward for her humorous cartoons, Anita Roddam for the ribbons, Sarah Giblett for the iconic image of the girl in the bed, used here and in the competition publicity; also for the bookmark design. Particular thanks to Miriam Sturdee for her delightful illustrations and cover, and for the overall design of the book. We are deeply grateful to Sarah MacBean, our publishing volunteer, whose skills, dedication and boundless enthusiasm have kept us on track throughout the whole process. Her immense hard work has made this book a reality.

We are grateful to the Co-operative Membership Community Fund for kindly funding this project.

Contents

## Imagine...								**33**

## Judgements								**47**

## Endurance								**61**

Poetry index

Poems by and for children

Humorous poems

Introductory Notes

ME/CFS

The illness, ME/CFS, has gone by many names. In the UK, 'ME' (Myalgic Encephalomyelitis) has been used mainly by sufferers, while the medical profession has used 'CFS' (Chronic Fatigue Syndrome), although this term also includes people who have less severe forms of fatiguing illness. 'ME/CFS' is used throughout this introduction. We have kept whatever term has been used by individual contributors.

OMEGA

Oxfordshire ME Group for Action (OMEGA) is the support and campaign group for people with ME, CFS and related conditions in Oxfordshire, UK.

For more information about ME/CFS and OMEGA see pages 99-101.

Blue Ribbon for ME/CFS

The blue ribbon is the international symbol for ME/CFS awareness.

Introduction

You probably know someone with ME or Chronic Fatigue Syndrome, but do you know what it is *really* like? We would like to let you into the world of the person with ME/CFS – to see the view 'from the bed' through original and powerful poetry.

These poems by adults and children beautifully express the reality of living with ME/CFS, both for sufferers and their families and friends: the struggle and determination, hope and despair, sadness and humour – above all the imagination and creativity of people living with this serious illness.

They are for

– everyone who loves poetry – and those who are not so sure
– anyone who would like to learn more about ME/CFS
– people with ME/CFS and their families, friends and carers.

Why this book?

Poems can say in a few well-chosen words what we know to be true, in a different or surprising way. Many people find poetry helpful or uplifting in dealing with difficult situations and it can provide enlightenment or give solace. There are poems in this book for different occasions and moods – from the poignant to the hopeful, to the ridiculously funny.

People who are house-bound with ME/CFS were not able to come to our poetry readings or exhibition in May 2012 and one of the aims of this book is to reach out to those who are at home, in bed.

Many people with ME/CFS have never met another person with the illness and may get little understanding from others. We hope this book will help lessen the isolation. Support groups like OMEGA (Oxfordshire ME Group for Action) are so important, enabling people to keep in touch with others via whatever means they can use: newsletter, website, Facebook or Twitter, phone calls or social events. People gain support and make friends, as well as learning about the latest research and treatments.

For those who do not have ME/CFS, we hope that these poems will enable you to better understand what having this illness is really like.

In my experience of talking to hundreds of people with ME/CFS, one issue that constantly arises is the lack of belief and understanding about the illness from some quarters – sometimes even from the people who might be expected to provide the most support; unfortunately this includes some doctors. Since OMEGA first started in 1989, things have improved, in that ME/CFS is much more readily accepted and understood. However, there is still prejudice and misunderstanding, which we hope this book will help to overcome.

OMEGA poetry competition

Poetry speaks from the heart, and it may seem surprising that we chose the medium of a competition to encourage people to express something so personal. We built on the experience of holding a successful art competition and exhibition in 2010, and knew that this could encourage members to be creative. We wanted to give people an opportunity to express how their life with ME/CFS *really* is. Poetry is personal both for the writer and the reader, and we are aware that our judge's choice may not be your choice of a favourite poem. You may like a poem that speaks to your direct experience, or perhaps expresses something about ME/CFS that you did not know before; as well as including the delight we can all take in beautifully expressed phrases and vivid imagery. Your favourite may change from one day to the next, and we hope that the variety of themes, styles and lengths will provide a poem for every occasion.

The competition did encourage a great many people to write poems. It inspired them to be creative and express themselves – it has awakened more than one person to the delights of both reading and writing poetry. Some people said that they had not written poetry before, and found it gave them a sense of achievement – which can be elusive for people with ME/CFS, owing to the limitations of extreme exhaustion and illness. We hope this book inspires more people to be creative and have a go themselves, as well as enjoying the fantastic poems we have here for you.

The competition was open to all, and advertised widely. This meant that people not connected with OMEGA saw our publicity, and, perhaps reminded of friends, colleagues or students who did have ME/CFS, were able to express their thoughts and feelings about it in poetry.

The poems written by children included here bring a particularly fresh, honest and moving slant to the theme – whether the child has ME/CFS themselves or observes the illness in their friend or parent.

We were absolutely delighted with the strength and variety of the entries – both from our members, and from other poets and well-wishers.

The exhibition and other events

ME/CFS Awareness Day is May 12th – focusing on the reality of life for people with ME/CFS, and the need for rigorous biomedical research. Events take place throughout the world on this day, and for the whole of May. We need to raise awareness in this way, as unfortunately the illness is still not well understood. This can lead to unjust treatment, particularly for children.

Incidentally, May 12th is also Limerick Day (the birthday of Edward Lear, the famous limerick writer) – very apt for our poetry events!

You will see, throughout this book, crossed ribbons representing the blue ribbons now adopted internationally as the symbol for ME/CFS Awareness. This blue ribbon was the starting point for the *45,000 Installation* which was devised by Anita Roddam to represent people with severe ME and to help achieve recognition.

She says:

Getting a name for my condition and illness in 1987, after 7 years of undiagnosed ME, had been a really momentous day at a very personal level. I had felt validated and believed after years of character assassination, and hostility from most quarters. Now, hearing of an international awareness campaign felt just as significant – but at a global level.

vii

On the same day, I heard the terms 'severely affected' and '25% ME Group' for the first time. For years I had been unable to read much from the journals of the main ME support groups because I was too ill... but in the 25% group everyone was virtually house-bound and/or bed-bound. Many were 100% bed-bound like myself.

It is important to make clear that this was written in 1998 and, particularly as a result of general government policy, nothing of benefit has changed. Although disbelief in the physical (biological) nature of ME and the requirement to justify have become harsher.

In the installation, the ribbon has been chosen to represent those people hidden from view, suffering from ME at home. This showed very movingly the huge number of people with severe ME, who are bed-bound or house-bound, and who are isolated from the ordinary world – at that time thought to be 45,000. Current estimates put the number of people with severe ME in the UK at approximately 63,000. Each person with ME is represented by a ribbon, and the effect of seeing page after page of the hand-drawn 'ribbons' graphically illustrates those with ME hidden from public awareness.

Anita says:

When I look at the installation I see many references:

– It reminds me of a War Memorial – and we are battling daily.
– I think of prisoners crossing off the days they have been confined, counting up until their release.
– I see graffiti, a wall of friendship, a petition, a protest, a vote of confidence.

viii

The 45,000 Installation is a touring exhibition, to which visitors are invited to contribute or comment. If you are interested in possibly hosting it as a group or even to have it in your own home, please contact: enquire.omega@gmail.com

One of the 45 pages of 1000 ribbons from the 45,000 Installation by Anita Roddam. Each ribbon represents one person who is bed-bound or house-bound with ME.

We curated an art and poetry exhibition in Oxford for the whole of May 2012. This included entries from the competition, and the 45,000 Installation. We also had a well-attended prize giving and poetry reading, and seven other readings throughout Oxfordshire during May. The installation and competition did a great deal towards awareness raising. Members of the public commented: 'Very moving poems', 'Fab Installation! Great poems!', 'Very moving – and important to bring to attention how many people have this condition and have to live with it for years'.

The poems

Life with ME/CFS has many different aspects, which are reflected in the poems. We have divided the book into themes, to help you choose which particular poem to read on any occasion. Obviously there are some overlaps, and many poems make reference to more than one theme. They are roughly in the order in which people experience their illness. In addition to including them in the main themes, we have also indicated which are the humorous poems and which are by and for children so that you can find these quickly.

Jan Seed
OMEGA

The Prize-Winning Poems
and Judge's Comments

We were extremely lucky to have as our judge for the poetry competition Vivien Steels, a published poet and artist, with personal experience of ME/CFS. She lives in Nottingham and did not know any of the entrants or their writing before. This meant we were able to have a completely independent judge, though unfortunately we have not been able to meet her in person, as she was too ill to travel to award the prizes. She wrote:

I really enjoyed reading ALL THE POEMS and thought the Adult and Omega member poems a very good standard with [the winner] being outstanding.

Vivien says:

I have written poetry since the early age of seven (I can still remember the poem I wrote then) and have loved poetry all my life. I have ME (or CFS/Chronic Fatigue Syndrome) and frequently have very little physical energy, but try to use my writing and painting as creative ways of counteracting this negativity.

Writing is an activity that requires a minimum of physical effort – you can do it anywhere, but it specially lends itself to bed, where I reside quite a lot of the time. I prop myself up with an architecture of pillows, until I disappear amongst large, white marshmallows, then I draw my feet up so that my legs form a natural support for my pad of paper.

There were three categories in the poetry competition: adult, up to 18 years old, and OMEGA members only.

The winning poems (comments by Vivien Steels)

1st prize adult – 'Anstice' (page 89)

In the poem 'Anstice', by Rosemary Johnson, the poet has created a rhyming poem, but the rhyming is so subtle you don't notice it and it often includes partial rhyming – very effective. She (or could be a 'he', though from the imagery I think a 'she') is observing her sister ill in bed with ME. I love the imagery, including a 'small pointed face', 'draining and featureless land of ME', 'like a fog or a blackout it smothers... Spreading a twilight', '...she grows slender and long/Like a Michaelmas daisy: reared without sunlight', 'dormant beneath the thick silt of fatigue/A spark yet remains', and ending with the wonderful line, 'And the soul and laughter are still in her eyes'. I felt I got to know Anstice the person from this poem and had the feeling that the writer is very close to her. I was wrapped up in this world while reading it. Brilliant!

2nd prize adult – 'In Memory of David's Sofa' (page 25)

'In Memory of David's Sofa' by Michelle Marsiglia, is a haunting poem (another rhyming one) imparting with strong poetic imagery what it is like to live with ME and how isolating the illness can be. We have the imagery of the foetus curled up (the position taken when under stress) but here it is strangely allied with ageing and the passage of time. The sufferer is 'a catatonic ghost' trying to cope 'without a handrail' or 'a guide dog that limps'. Even a guide dog in this world is disabled. Confined to the sofa (I know this feeling) the writer feels 'I'm already too late'. Too late for life? For getting going on that day or every day? For dreams of doing what she would like to do? The last verse is so strong. 'Sloth' is a very ugly word, and no ME sufferer is lazy, but that awful inaction ME engenders is ugly. The sofa has metaphorically given way under the weight of someone lying on it all day. The last two lines are fantastic – 'And the day has transformed/Into a grey shade of moth'. 'Grey' is a depressing shade and also heralds the night and, combined with a night-creature, 'moth', we, the reader, get a hopeless, fluttery sort of going-nowhere-feeling – just like an ME relapse.

1st prize OMEGA – 'Dormant Garden' (page 79)

I loved the simplicity of this poem by Patricia Wells, which uses the imagery of the natural world with such ease to emphasise the hibernatory aspect of ME. Who hasn't hidden away under their duvet on a bad ME day or for weeks, months at a time? BUT it is a poem full of fertile metaphors in the last 4 lines of the first verse – 'Under my duvet of leaf-litter./Roots still alive/Fed by green memory,/Compost of my lively past'. This is writing at its simplest and best. These images link us to the possibility of the reviving aspects of hope encompassed in the coming of Spring, but will the writer be well enough to join in the burgeoning new life? There is always hope and this is such a lovely, hopeful poem.

xiii

2nd prize OMEGA – 'Words, or the Woman with ME Tries to Write a Poem' (page 20)

Jan Seed's poem centres on her love of words. I loved the originality of this poem. It is 'wordy' but in a good, creative and unique way. We have puns in the first verse – page/blankly, pencil/leadenly, computer mouse/squeaked. The second verse opens up into full-blown poetic expression with three beautiful descriptive lines 'sparkled like early morning sun on a shimmering spider-web dew', 'shiny new conker, snug in its milky-white cushion', 'sun-warmed wood of a well-turned walking stick' (which reminds us of disability again). Then, in the third and fourth verse, the dreaded ME brain fog descends and reason goes haywire with 'thingy' being the term for everything you can't find the elusive name for. I loved the concrete poetry where the words actually 'slithered down the page into a heap on the floor'. And so does the poet! Original, witty and fun with a serious message about the impact of ME on our mental capacities.

1st prize up to 18 years – 'ME' (page 26)

This poem by Tao Mitchell, who is nine years old, shows with such directness (the directness of a child) helped by the repetition of 'ME, ME' and the same structure for each verse, what an *awful* illness ME is and how it affects children.

All the main symptoms and effects are there:
1. Living with this illness every day
2. How life after ME will never be the same

3. It isn't visible to others but causes so much pain both physically and emotionally

4. It results in real strain and stress in one's life

This is a very good poem that tells the reader so much about the illness ME in very few words.

2nd prize up to 18 years – 'Bed' (page 15)

'Bed' by Louis Garden, aged seven, is a very brave poem, which highlights not only the unrelenting exhaustion of ME in the refrain at the beginning and end of the poem: 'bed, tired, asleep, wake up, tired again', but also the problem of wetting the bed, which is twice as common in boys and happens when children are unwell, under stress or having sleep problems and we all know what stress ME puts the body under and how our sleep is disrupted.

I loved the complete honesty of the poem plus the clipped, short phrases which add to the feeling of stress and exhaustion. Again a poem which says in few words so much about ME.

Vivien Steels
Talking Paint
www.viviensteels.webs.com

How My Life Changed

ME/CFS can affect anyone of any age, gender or ethnic origin; and from all walks of life. Before the illness people mostly led ordinary lives: they went to school or work, had active social lives, and enjoyed activities such as dancing, hill-walking or fishing ('Fishing Before and After ME/CFS'). When we lose all this it can be a shock, especially when someone becomes ill suddenly; it has a profound effect. In the poems in this first section we learn about the earlier life of the person with ME/CFS and how this has now changed ('Loss'), and how people have managed to adapt to their new life ('Half Life').

How My Life Changed

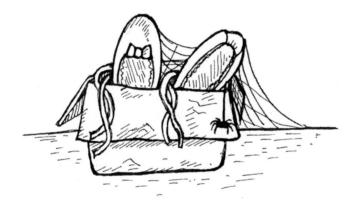

Spring Fever

Here's April's Spring fever,
I wait eagerly for
My body to respond
As once it did.

With the brightening light
My mind expands,
Emotions become buoyant
Hope rises with new growth.

Alas, the rising energy
Is not matched, and like
A plant that's suffered
Frost damage, I remain.

As before.

Lynda Holland

Half Life

I remember days gone by
When I was fit – and then I sigh,
A working mum with a house so clean
Lifts for the kids wherever they'd been

Ballroom and Latin one night a week,
Quiz on a Sunday the answers to seek,
Friday was town night, dancing 'til late
2am when I came in the gate!

Round at my sister's or friend's for a chat,
Now I have to forget about that,
Fog has descended upon my poor brain,
My body is aching, it's all such a drain

My batteries are low for much of the day
I'm basically sleeping my life away,
The urge to have fun has gone I'm afraid,
I just want to rest, so indoors I have stayed.

Tomorrow's a challenge – what will it bring?
I never can tell, I can't plan a thing.
My life has been altered over the years
ME has brought me some sadness and tears

But now that I know what I can and can't do
I know what's required to help me get through
I often find that I'm not understood,
Regarded as 'strange' – I'd change if I could!

My energy levels have all gone to pot,
But it's no use complaining and whining a lot
I've got it – this 'half life' – but have to go on
So that's what I'll do 'til the cure comes along.

Samantha Pike

She and ME

She climbs a mountain,
I climb the stairs.
She runs for the bus,
I run a bath.
She meets friends for coffee and chat,
I check emails in bed.
She cleans the house in a whirlwind,
I wash up.
She follows her career path,
I potter down the garden path.
She plans a world trip,
I plan a hospital trip.
She lives life to the full,
I watch life pass by.

Lucy Stone

It's ME but it's Not *Me*

I'm so lonely inside, tired of being blue
I want the old me back and so do you.
This isn't the me I want to be. Too young to be old.
But my body has another story to be told.

Seeing people laughing, running, and playing make me sad,
and because I can't always do those things I feel very bad.
This illness is like a thief.
It came in the one night and has brought me nothing but grief.
I yearn for the days of the past.
Times when my life was filled with joy, laughter, and hope.
Now it seems all I do is cry, get mad, or mope.
Sorry my love for the pain and frustration this has brought.
I hate all the lessons this illness has taught.

Daphne Oxley

Fishing Before and After ME/CFS

Fishing, my hobby for thirty-five of my forty-seven years, any spare time I had was mostly in the pursuit of predators, it used to be an enjoyable challenge. Now it's more like an endurance test.

I used to fish internationally, nationally and locally. Now only locally on a good day.

Before I could get up before dawn and go, now it takes me several hours to stabilise/prepare myself for a trip. I will not last long.

I would fish in all weather conditions, now only fair conditions on a good day.

Tackle was carried miles, around a pit, lake or along a riverbank. Now only a few metres, it used to feel light, now it feels heavy.

Lure fishing was at times dawn till dusk, the rod held all day, teasingly working the lure to attract a predator. Now I only seem to last a few minutes, and end up with aching limbs and the onset of tendonitis.

After a trip I would return home recharged, relaxed, no ill effects and ready for anything. Now I return home a shattered, seized-up, rundown, slowed wreck that can take weeks to recover.

If I wasn't fishing I was often thinking about ways to improve, now I'm thinking of ways to improve my health.

When I feel well enough to go fishing I seem to make myself worse – a catch 22.

The Fisherman

Loss

Loss of health
Loss of freedom
Loss of movement
Loss of talent
Loss of friends
Loss of sleep
Loss of memory
Loss of a future?

Sylvia Booth

Brain Fog and Other Symptoms

In this section, the poems focus on individual symptoms, particularly *brain fog*. This is extreme mental exhaustion – where thinking, reading, or even talking becomes impossible and attempts can provoke relapse. People may have great difficulty in finding the right word ('Words') or even any words at all.

People with ME/CFS are often very sensitive to light, sound and temperature and are very often intolerant of alcohol, scented products and some foods ('Lady Light', 'I Take a Sip').

Symptoms including pain and fatigue ('Me CFS Limerick'); or a combination of symptoms such as sleep disturbance and bed-wetting ('Bed') are the focus of some poems here.

Poems throughout the book mention some of the many symptoms, including extreme exhaustion, pain, headache, dizziness and digestive disorders, that often form part of life with ME/CFS.

Brain Fog and Other Symptoms

ME Haiku

I was writing a Haiku
on ME
when along came brain-fog and...

Sandra Fardon Fox

Lady Light

The wavelength of light,
Is ever so slight,
One hundredth the width,
Of a human hair,
It's almost as if,
You're not really there.

My tastebuds don't dance,
To any sort of tune,
Played by the sunlight,
Bounced from the moon.

No colourful cacophony,
Can be heard by my ears,
I see your game,
You freak! You Queer!

Oh, but Lady Light,
I love you so much!
But like a cheap peepshow,
I can look, but not touch.

Nathan Smith

14

Bed

Bed, tired, asleep, wake up, tired again.
Resting in my bed, oh dear I've wet my BED!!!!
Come out tired and wet, change pyjamas
Move to sofa
I miss my bed
Bed, tired, asleep, wake up, tired again.

Louis Garden, age 7

I Take a Sip

I take a sip of wine
Find a fish scale lodged between my teeth
Causing gum to bleed and nerve ending to tingle sharply
The shapes in my coffee begin to look like strange countries
Things I haven't seen or tasted before
Places I will never visit and never call home

I begin to observe details within the landscape
Like elephant skin it ages nicely
And as I hum to the sound of madness
Making sounds without pitch or potency
The negative becomes the narrative
Of someone's attempt at poetry

Distorted children haunt the corners collecting dust
They speak of distortion and childhood and racket and
resonance
Leaving out words that mean the most to those ignorant
enough to feel them
Those who haven't withered away with thought
Those who are fully alive and understand the earth well
Those whose parting words will be louder than fireworks

More can be said without reference
Matters can be solved when dried out in scorching heat
When left in mirky pools to stagnate and bloat up like bodies
Of relatives you've never heard of and debts gone unpaid
They swim up to the surface to feed
Little mouths greedy for things too large to swallow

I would have you choke on this noise
I would have it seething out of every exit
Pushing against the systems within
Convulsing and being very unhappy
Because it needs space to breathe deeply
It needs what tobacco smothers up

The wine goes down slowly after that first gulp
Hesitant and wary to what might come next
It eyes me up from below
Wondering how much I'm worth, how strong I am
Where I was made and if I'm worth the sacrifice
Then fingers its pockets for loose change

The taste of iron isn't leaving any time soon
Its coarse texture leaves me hoarse and cracked
And it speaks in tongues that must be foreign
For my own tongue is deaf to the incessant rantings
Of this red-faced pirate
That can't hold his drink

I humanize machinery
And make everything look the same
Bring something in
And give it all the same pallet
I remove nostalgia from distance
Inject absence into colour.

Constantine Alexander Blintzios

Me CFS Limerick

My Chronic Fatigue is so tiring.
The symptoms are less than inspiring.
From brain-fog to pain,
They're all such a drain.
It's like I need total rewiring!

Sandra Fardon Fox

Untitled (Descartes said)

Descartes said: I think, therefore I am.
I think, but do not know my thoughts,
Therefore I am not?

Anita Roddam

Words, or the Woman with ME Tries to Write a Poem

She stared at the page.
Blankly.
She sucked on the pencil.
Leadenly.
The pen had the blues
And wouldn't write.
At the computer, she touched the pad.
The mouse squeaked.
The caps locked with the key.

She wanted words!
Words –
That sparkled like early morning sun on shimmering spider-web dew.
Words –
With the apt perfection of a shiny new conker, snug in its
milky-white cushion.
Words –
Like the sun-warmed wood of a well-turned walking stick,
Reflecting years of craft and handling.

Instead, when exhaustion slammed into her body and brain,
Crushing and mangling all in its wake,

'*Thingy*', the perpetual understudy, stuttered on a deserted stage;
'*TV remote*' lay bound and gagged in the wings,
While '*the blue thing*' (it *is* black, of course),
And even '*courgette*' auditioned for the part.

Meanwhile, poor '*bread knife*' fell down a crack in the floorboards,
Down into the hidden murky depths,
And an exasperated mime artist sawed vainly in the empty air.

The slippery words *sLuRred* and *sli*

                        ther

                            ed

                                        d

                                          o

                                            w

                                              n

                                            the page

                                                into
                                              a heap
                                            on the floor.

                                            And so did she.

Jan Seed

Getting Through the Day

People with ME/CFS are survivors: they develop all sorts of strategies to get through the day, even though this can be a big struggle. The poems in this section are unflinching in their accurate reflection of how much of an unending trial this can be ('Wake Up', 'Untitled (Exhausted)'); although some days may be better than others, with 'good days' and bad days' ('So You Have ME').

One of the main coping techniques is pacing: living life in 'bite-size chunks'. Pacing means having to stop enjoyable or necessary activities half-way through for a rest, and curtailing activities that will cause relapse. This is not easy, and can be very frustrating, as people with ME/CFS long to be active.

Getting Through
the Day

In Memory of David's Sofa

I curl back into an orphan
Cradling a place
Where my body ages
Subtle, like the spinning of the earth

Foetal composure
Limbs engrossed
A small space taken up
By a catatonic ghost

Human vision;
An indent on the world's perception
Coming to terms and getting to grips
Without a handrail to support
Or a guide dog that limps

May I please confide
In this prostrate state
That the hour is lending
And I'm already late

The sofa has sunk
Capsized under sloth
And the day has transformed
Into a grey shade of moth

Michelle Marsiglia

25

ME

ME
What I live with every day

ME
ME
My life will never be the same

ME
ME
Can't see it but there's pain

ME
ME
My life is full of strain

Tao Mitchell, age 9

Untitled (Exhausted, I sink down)

Exhausted, I sink down in the chair.
So much I should be doing but I have no strength.
My limbs quiver with fatigue.
Energy has left my body.
It is almost an effort to breathe.
I am tired, so very tired.
I have been claimed by Morpheus.
An unwilling bride wrapped tightly in his arms.
The urge to lie down, to rest, to sleep is insatiable.
Will I ever shake off the embrace?

This poem is about my experience of exhaustion. Although I don't have ME, I know someone who does. I imagine this is what it is like.

Susy Bohrer

Wake Up

tired... headache... exhausted...   the day has just begun

Lunch Time

not moved... muscle pain... headache...   the day is half done

Dinner Time

can't think... things need to be done...
still in bed, curtains closed... only moved to go to the bathroom

Bed Time

The day is now done... let's hope tomorrow is a
different day

Tracy Gibson

Poem About Myalgic Encephalomyelitis

ME is so exhaust..

Joanna Breheny

So You Have ME

You have muscle weakness,
You have exhaustion,
You have pain.
But you have four walls upstairs,
Four walls downstairs
And a bit of the garden,
If you are lucky –
On a good day.

You cannot walk far,
You cannot think straight,
You cannot talk long.
But you have a bed upstairs,
A settee downstairs
And a bit of concentration,
If you are lucky –
On a good day.

You have an ignorant GP,
You have an arrogant Consultant,
You have negative tests.
But you have a radio upstairs,
A television downstairs
And a book to read,
If you are lucky –
On a good day.

Today is a bad day.

Vivien Steels

Imagine...

About half of our members are house-bound or can hardly ever go out. They are unable ever to come to OMEGA events. People who are very ill try many different methods to enable them to deal with the life they have. Some find solace in turning within, perhaps in meditation ('Autumn Meditation'). Many use their imaginations to replace the world that they are cut off from ('Duvet Dreamtime'). Some go on 'virtual holidays' where they imagine themselves in different countries, or on adventures ('The Bed'); or go to 'virtual parties' where they put on their best pyjamas and play non-active games, such as dead lions ('Professional'). Others may make up stories to amuse themselves ('ME and a Mouse').

Imagine...

33

Untitled
(Bury me in the Deep Goodnight)

Bury me in the Deep Goodnight of Stars
Streaming across the sky
Their path to dawn slides to a fade

My heart soars as satellites pass
Dreams colliding with
All that has come to pass

My heart will sing
I will lift my soul
I will it so

To be beautiful in spite of all grim
All I have been forced to factor in

I will be deeply embroidered
Canvas, Textured, Brilliant, New.

Nin

An Unfortunate Man with ME

An unfortunate man with ME
For a cure sat on top of a tree
'Though it's really quite frightening
at least there's no 'lightning'
and it's better than C.B.T.

David Polgreen

CBT (Cognitive Behaviour Therapy) and Lightning Process are controversial
psychological treatments sometimes used for people with ME/CFS

Is it Today?

Is it today that I dream no more?
As I look at the bag lying there by the door.

Forget that dream of climbing those hills?
Turning to gasp and feeling such thrills.
That fresh green grass, that clear blue sky.
The tinkling of bells as the cows wander by.

Just one more mile then back for tea.
I tighten the laces and set off with glee.
No tiredness, no brain fog, certainly no pain.
No stopping to rest again and again.

Passing beautiful houses, Geraniums galore.
Kaffee und Kuchen, mmm – need I say more?
Evening meal, then dancing till two.
Straight into bed and sleeping right through.

I gaze at my boots lying there in the box.
Long strong laces, good thick socks.
Do I finally part with them, send them away?
Give in to ME and call it a day?

Shall I give up the dream of walking one day
on those beautiful hills miles away?

Yes, I've decided. It's really okay.
They will go to charity.
But just not today!

Jo Porter

Duvet Dreamtime

What time is it? I hear you ask.
It's tomorrow, I reply.
Tomorrow already...? Really?

But it doesn't matter.
We have all the time in the world,
In Duvet Dreamtime.

Instead of the damp and the slugs and the din
We can dream of comfort

In the house with the garden
We'll have when we move...

Instead of us working,
We can dream we're on holiday

In the garden of the house,
We'll have when we move...

Instead of being too ill to move
We can dream we take
One step

In the garden of the house
We'll have, when we move...

Instead of this isolation
We can dream we are cherished

In the house with the garden,
We'll have when we move...

Instead of my daughter in care
We can dream we're together

In the house with the garden
We'll have when we move...

What day is it? I ask you.
It's Egg Day, you say,
I know, because I just counted them...

But it doesn't matter.
We have all the time in the world.
It's still Duvet Dreamtime, you know.

Paula Butler

Autumn Meditation

(dedicated to my meditation teacher: Dido Dunlop)

I lie me down in tired gold
with fading greens, retreating reds,
crisping from the outside in
and seeping back to wood and dark

I hold the bright light in my depth
as winter's firelight dreams of spring,
remember where the stories are
and seek the universe within

My body aches, I sense my breath
my pillowed head, my legs, my chest
my skin becomes translucent thin
the tide of gentle black rising –
and shining orbs float out released:
I take my rest in spaciousness

Cassandra Wall

Professional

I'm in training
I train for hours each day
My sport is 'Dead Lions'
I'll aim for the Olympics
But I won't win
I need the loo too often.

Zoë Williams

Dead Lions is a children's party game along the lines of 'who can lie completely still for the longest?'.

The Bed

with apologies to A. A. Milne

Christopher Robin and a bear named Pooh
Are probably well known to you.
I liked his poem called 'Nursery Chairs',
I even liked the one about bears.

I lie in bed, I dream and stare,
Just as he did from his chair.
Each of the chairs, it was his stage
Amazon, ship, and lion's cage.

1.
When I go up the Amazon
I listen to the bird's bright song –
I simply stop and stand.
And butterflies in twos and threes
Come silently between the trees.
I wait for them to land.
And chainsaws heard from far away?
I'll deal with them another day –
They really should be banned!
With earplugs in, then come what may
I will enjoy this land.

2.

I'm a great big bear with a big sore head,
And I often frighten people with a groan.
Then I put on a brave face, and
Tell them not to be so frightened –
And they don't be so frightened any more.

3.

When I am in my ship, I see
The lovely clouds go sailing by.
A real ship would just make me
As sick, as sick – so I just lie
Pretending here that I'm at sea:
The world is sailing by.
I can go all around the world
Without a how or why.

4.

At last, at the end of the day's thread,
So tired that I'm ready to weep,
I try to pretend that it's my bed
And that I will get a good sleep.

Jan Seed

If I Woke Up Well

If I woke up well
Would I recognise myself,
Or think 'Who is this?'

David Polgreen

ME and a Mouse

I'm not very good at walking, not even into a house. My ME says I'm tired – I must stay in bed and oh, I'm Muffity Mouse. My diary shows I lived in a field of green but all that changed. It did when the crop-circles came, and then it rained and rained. Soaked, so wet I struggled to find a home, then found one of steel. Some called it a silly steel tube but kindly folk said it were a pink submarine. For fun I flew the Jolly Roger from my bed all night, until those imaginary sailors slyly put out the light. In my bed, down I go, and all below the sea, the blue sky has gone, and upside down is that vast carpet, to me of bright pea green. One day I'll struggle home where ole church bells ring. When that happens I'll be looking for a gold band for my wife, perhaps that diamond for the King. Hurrah for the local pub where I taste the cider brew, me Dear, then I'm off to the old belfry and me so full of fear. I've heard many country tales, the clever ones chill me bones, and from underneath my bed comes a ghostly rattling of the stones. And think ye on me scarecrow Chum, you stand there with a face like Hell, can't decide to leave the field, or when and who to tell. Old faithful Scarecrow join me for a drink as is only fair, for with his ME all his life he's spent, empty face and arms outstretched, looking up into the air. I see the blackbirds come to peck at him and then his straw to chew but would they do that if he could walk? Seems only ME and I knew.

Cleveland W. Gibson

Judgements

ME/CFS is confusing, to everyone. It is difficult to understand, especially as people may look perfectly well on days they are well enough to go out ('When You Look at Me'). What you don't see is their long hours spent recovering after a trip out or even a short visit from a friend. People with ME/CFS are ill, not just tired; this isn't laziness ('Can't Find Sympathy') or depression ('The Story of a Geordie Girl'). The over-hasty judgements of others, and the struggle to explain and justify themselves, as well as coping with the illness itself, can cause immense distress. We hope people will listen to people with ME/CFS and try to understand what they are going through – to 'put yourself in someone else's shoes' ('Judgement'). The difficulties of obtaining benefits can cause additional stress and exhaustion ('Testing, Testing').

Judgements

Don't Ask Me

Don't ask me if I'm tired
It makes no sense to me
Fatigued? Exhausted?
Doesn't mean a thing
On my planet
Gravity's ten times stronger,
On my planet
A diver's lead boots are on my feet,
On my planet
The air's too thin,
On my planet
A glass of water weighs a ton.
So don't ask me if I'm tired
I won't know what
You're on about.
I might just punch you
Right on the nose –
If I had the strength!

Lynda Holland

ME by Me

My head aches, I feel so tired,
My young body seems unwired,
Like a puppet whose strings have been cut,
Exhausted, too tired to get up.

I was fit once, so full of life,
No anticipation of this kind of strife.
I had a job, it meant more than you could tell.
But I couldn't cope, lost it, entered hell.

No one wants me, so it appears,
Nobody shares my endless fears.
Wheelchair-bound, losing my voice,
No one wants this if they had the choice.

Please, please try to understand,
I want to be like you, hold my hand.
Help me to come through this ME
To live my life as it should be.

No more 'Pull yourself together!'
I'll get through this spell of listless weather.
Feeling better now, nearing my journey's end
Of an illness which few can comprehend.

The light at the end of the tunnel beckons,
A horrible experience, over, I reckon.

Mervyn Powell

The Story of a Geordie Girl and Her Distress at the Hands of a Medical Professional and Why is the Title Longer Than the Poem?

There was a young lass from the Tyne
Who was pretty and witty and kind
She said 'Deary me
I think it's ME.'
Her Doc said 'It's all in your mind!'

John Porter

A Fashionable Disease

I didn't think anyone would be
remotely interested
in a poem about ME

'It's a very *fashionable* disease.'
– Really?
I suppose we wear it well;
Like a coat of spikes
or a bed of nails.
It's like saying to
someone with cancer
'You're named after
an astrological sign.'
Or to someone with M.S.
'You must have multiple choices.'

No one who has –
fevered with flu,
felt hugely hungover,
run five miles just
to get to the bathroom,

blacked out merely
by standing up,
lain in bed
unable to move,
had the pain of incessant neuralgia
flashing though each muscle –
nerves perpetually tortured –
could liken such a devastating destroyer
of all that is taken for granted
by the wholistically healthy
as *fashionable*.

I'd like them to experience
the catwalk of catastrophe
for a day – or perhaps until
time turns its light-framed tables
and a different style of pain emerges
for another person to eternally endure.

Vivien Steels

Can't Find Sympathy

A poem by a Chronic Fatigue Syndrome sufferer

What do you see
When you look at me...
The words on your lips are nothing but lies
I see the disgust in your unloving eyes

I can't find sympathy

This heavy weight presses me down
Squeezes the tears from a tired non-clown
The aches and pains don't go away
I just can't move – I'm ashamed to say

I can't find sympathy

If my body was broken and twisted in pain
Would your sympathy then be mine to gain
I lie in a bed not to sleep or dream
This isn't laziness – is my silent scream
CFS is an illness that you don't understand
But I'm still me so why won't you **please** *just hold my hand*

I Can't Find Sympathy

Linda Angeletta

Testing, Testing

You can be 'idle' at Lent,
Without being indolent,
You can be a grafter at heart,
Whose brain just won't start,
You can be bed-ridden all day,
When your hair isn't grey,
You can be put to the test,
When you're groggy and stressed,
You can be told to 'get on your bike'
Without a chance to strike,
You can be told to contribute more,
When you're struggling and poor,
You can use 'lazy' preconceptions,
Which you never question,
You can take time to understand,
Offer careful, considered plans,
You can judge a disability?
When it isn't plain to see.

James Matejtschuk

When You Look at Me, What Do You See?

When you look at me
What do you see?

When you look at me
what you don't see
Is a woman who has always flown in the face of adversity
I picked myself up, time after time
I brushed myself down
I started all over again

You certainly don't see the me with ME
I'm smiling, I'm laughing, I'm listening to you
I'm sorry you're poorly, what can I do?

A few minutes later – the room starts to swim
the legs go weak and the lights grow dim
The noise gets so loud, I can no longer think straight
I feel startled and jumpy at six's and eight's
My words come out wrong, I speak gobbledy-gook
The people around me they're starting to look

The stick that I hold is not just for show
It really is my support when my life-force starts to go

I refuse to give in, I know I should be good
But this occasional outing is important to me!
My world is so small when it should be so big
I'm breaking the rules,
Do I give a fig?

Well actually yes I really do care
but I'm between a rock and a hard place, insanity or despair.

So when I come for my pills or to pick up a book,
It's because I feel brave and devil may care,
It may not last long
but at least I was there

I know I exist, I do matter still
It's me with ME not a shadow that's ill!

Jayne Diston

57

Judgement

Subject of distain,
some people can't refrain
from espousing
their 'cure' and crude views.

It's ever open season,
for there has to be a reason –
psychological? lazy? the blues?

Where the compassion?
Is it really out of fashion
to put yourself in someone else's shoes?

Sue Taylor

What's in a Name...?

I was a Burden
Before we married.
Now I fear I have become
What my name predicted

Freya Morris (née Burden)

Endurance

ME/CFS can be a very long-lasting illness and sometimes there is nothing to do but endure the pain and exhaustion. In 'Endurance', the endless struggle of people with ME/CFS is compared to the experience of the polar explorer Shackleton battling each step of the way. There is a sort of stoicism, or even denial, which leads to the ill person just 'doing the next thing' and putting on a brave face. Many poems refer to this bravery, and the refusal to give in.

Other poems show how the spark or spirit of the person is still there. A person is still themselves, even though they may not be able to be active. Through acceptance of what *is*, people can find joy, despite their suffering ('Pass This Way').

Endurance

Endurance

Shackleton, I watch Branagh play you
– from the comfort of my sofa
each step a struggle for life itself
– while I sit by my log fire
in the ultimate bleak and cold
– and I think: why?

Why put yourself through such feats
– when of necessity we with ME
battle each step of the day
with utter exhaustion, and against despair,
to make food, wash, and ease the pain
of mind and body in such extremity

But I understand you:
like you I will survive, against the elements
that oppress me – I know you:
across the years your struggle
helps me access that vital human spark –
I will endure: I am extraordinary.

*Kenneth Branagh played Ernest Shackleton for Channel 4's drama of
the true story of his journey in search of the South pole on board the
ship Endurance.*

Cassandra Wall

63

Poetry from the Bed:
Life with ME/CFS

Trapped on the turgid trampoline
Dying a duckdown death
Wrapped in a duvet November to May
Trying to hold your breath

Cry out in rage as they rattle your cage
Sigh for the waste of a life
Try not to age as you finish each page
Cryogenics might soften this strife

Anita Roddam

Pass This Way

Fly away life Fly away life
but not a die away life of
Final earth covered rest

Dreams Hopes Wants Needs Old Fears
Childhood to youth to grown-up years
Spent forming

All now
Smashed Turning and Falling to
Strange and frightening hues
Lost days lost dreams
Spent in weakness and fear.

It passes
It passes as all life passes
Strangely Weirdly Unbelievably
I Pass and Change and Shift and
Grow to new understanding

For now I sleep or rest or dream or suffer
In a new haze of understanding and
in this acceptance I grow and
Love and sometimes laugh.

My life is joy
The pain has moved
Me on.

Nin

Then

In school she was teaching,
Her peak she was reaching,
She worked day and night,
A headship in sight.

She ate five veg a day
Kept obesity at bay.
She looked really good,
As indeed she should

Then

Chronic Fatigue Syndrome.
She tried not to moan.
Barely could get up,
Tired, pouring tea in a cup.

Sitting in her wheelchair,
Strangers would often stare.
How long would this last?
Would it soon pass?

Months became years,
Too many tears.

Then

Never giving up hope,
She learnt how to cope.
She was no fool,
But she longed for her school.

Then

At long last
She was back with her class.

Hurray!

A tribute to one of my best students who survived ME.

Mervyn Powell

Looking Out

People with ME/CFS are forced to lead limited lives, often having to stay in bed or in their homes. Many find it extremely difficult to have social contact, no matter how much they want it, as it makes them too ill. When they are able to, they look out on ('From My Bed'), or perhaps only listen to ('The Street'), the outside world. However, the outside world cannot see in, and people with ME/CFS are hidden. The ill person themselves may start to feel invisible. In an average street of 60 houses, there is likely to be at least one person with ME/CFS, who may be unknown to their neighbours.

Occasionally, even people who are very ill may be able to venture out. The delight and excitement of this is well shown in 'The Journey'.

Looking Out

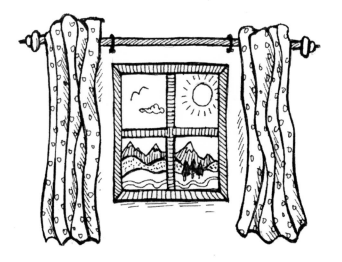

The Street

The street downstairs
Holds walking figures.
My neighbours
Chat, gossip, pass the time of day.
My room holds me
Prone, quiet, listening.

Patricia Wells

From My Bed...

From my bed, snowflakes past the window fall,
    cutlery scrapes, glasses chink,
      'Merry Christmas to you all!'

From my bed, springtime happiness fills the hall,
    lawnmowers start, kids laugh and play,
    courting birds coo and call.

From my bed, summer fragrance to enthral,
    the sunshine blazes in, barbeques sizzle,
    quiet fills the hall.

From my bed, clouds fill in and temperatures fall,
    fireworks flash, bang and boom,
    bonfire smoke and autumn leaves fall.

From my bed, where time stands still,
    another year passes...

Lucy Stone

The Journey

My home; beautiful village, wonderful country
Familiar but sparkling after my inside absence.
Eyes open more often than intended
Calculating how much wonder I can afford.
The car's good – a real bed!
I lie facing backwards
Looking straight at people behind.
They take me in their stride,
But I'm glad of my sunglasses.

Never such heat in my room –
My trip to the tropics!
Stopped with the boot open,
Loving the unfamiliar breeze.
Two car-parks with trees and birds
Unlike memories of lifeless tarmac.
A hand dryer blows warm air through my fingers,
Enough to amuse me for days;
But I must be disciplined,
Ear defenders and blindfold my essentials.

We took three hours over the ten-mile journey.
Short bursts and rests minimising the impact,
Inevitably growing more and more ill.
Two days later I'd recovered,
So relieved to be OK,
Ready for an incredible week.

Zoë Williams

Holidays

Countryside, sand, tea.
Some have spontaneity.
ME? – wait and see

Sue Taylor

Escape from Bed

A year ago I was fit and well. Now I'm stuck in bed, crying
through this ME Hell.

My head – it splits right in two, arms, legs and whole body
aches so what can I do?

I take the pills, rest a while, making no sense of it all
though I smile.

Sure, I've run, also swum in the bucking blue sea but that
was before ME.

To say it straight: I'm in a mess, energy gone, not too much
of that left I guess.

ME says the dice always reads low, it is random with only
Upwards the way to go.

With ME I dream in bed, draw figures, write words,
enough said.

I love colours to excite my mind, bright colours, red and
yellow, are the best kind.

Yet how to motivate my entire frame, eating food for
energy is never the same.

Something is wrong, that makes me slow, I forget a word,
not the best way to go.

Now listen up: have you a plan, a word of hope, or must I
sit still in bed and mope?

Sorry but I fear that option is not me. I'll even try music to
fool ME.

Bring on ABBA, Mozart, Barry, Elvis, Bolero, Porter and more.
Play LOUD music – if it means I'm first out of bed , then
out of that door!

Cleveland W. Gibson

Hope

Despite years of illness, there remains hope, and people *long to* recover ('Life with ME/CFS'). Many of the poems throughout the book reflect this. Some people do get a lot better ('Gone is the Winter of My Discontent'), and some may improve enough to be able to lead a more active life, even though they may always have to be careful with managing how much they do and getting enough rest. No-one knows who will improve or when – many of the poems raise questions about the future ('The Dance', 'Dormant Garden').

Hope

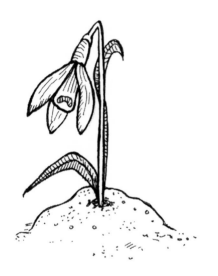

Dormant Garden

You can't see me
Tucked away
Under my duvet of leaf-litter.
Roots still alive
Fed by green memory,
Compost of my lively past.

You can't see me
Tucked away
Warm in the mid-winter.
Verdant, lively,
Will I join in spring
This year?

Patricia Wells

Life with ME/CFS

Body is cemented, cracking,
each limb swallowed by the bed.

Mind is shifting,
underwater and unfocusing

An arm slung over eyes,
shielding off the light.

The odd thoughts sweep in and out like weed.

Sitting up, oh Herculean effort,
causes the space to spin.

An attack of music from outside,
ending like a withdrawn fist,

I breathe, count my blessings,

smile.

I hope to recover,

I hope to return to life,

I hope,

I hope,

I hope.

Joanna Breheny

Gone is the Winter of My Discontent

It's January, and the cherry tree's in bloom.
It thinks it's cheated winter.
Birds sing in the dark afternoon:
For them mild weather tokens spring.
Twenty winters tolled my illness,
Hard, and never promising spring.
All seasons brought their hardship,
Hoping for hope that never came.
And then one April it came at last,
That scent of flowers, that rumour of some healing powers.
'Many are helped', my kind friend said.
'I think it might be just worth trying.
What's there to lose, but more despair –
The treatment's just so near to here.'

And so I went, and drank the draught,
Little thinking, little hoping, fearing failure, fearing loss,
Telling no one, feeling guilty.
Why should this work when nothing had?
But good can come from so much sorrow,
The treatment found by one who'd suffered –
Passionate now to spread the healing.
Green shoots in April brought my strength back,
Slowly, pacing, breathing, sensing, wellness, peace – a joyful feeling.

Susanna Geddes

The Dance

'Let's go to the dance today?'
'Oh yes, I'd love to' I would say.
Up the stairs two by two.
Which dress to wear?
Dark red or blue?

Out again come dancing shoes.
More decisions, which to choose?
Happily dancing the night away.
Sometimes seeing the light of day!

Years go by – feeling good –
as any 'healthy' person should!
Walking, climbing, yoga, gym.
Feeling great – and keeping slim!!!

Then into my life a stranger came.
Unwelcome guest, ME by name.
Aching head, muddled brain.
Body burning, lots of pain.

Feeling ill from day to day.
'Can't find a reason', the doctors say
Lots of tests, nothing shows.
'It could be ME... I suppose'.

Blue Badge, wheelchair, walking stick too.
Feet no longer straight and true.
What has happened, why to me?
What is this illness, this ME?

Time goes by, many years.
Lots of pain, lots of tears.
Sleepless nights with no reprieve.
When will this illness ever leave?

... Perhaps **this** year could be the one
when my unwelcome guest has gone.
Then maybe once again you'll say:
'Let's go to the dance today?'.

Jo Porter

In the Face Of...

Give me the strength, I pray to you,
To get inside my life
However small, it may be
And from there,
Look outwards at the delight in the world
And, through as many acts of kindness

As I can muster
Nurture those nuggets
To lighten up the bleakness
That too,
Is there.

Tonya Stevens

ME/CFS Affects Us All

ME/CFS affects many other people as well as the person who is ill. The impact of the illness on family and friends can be huge – not just when they are the carers, but also as sisters ('Anstice'), brothers, parents or children; and even friends of the family ('My Mum's Friend'). This is especially devastating for those who live with a person who has severe ME/CFS. The sibling of a child with ME/CFS has to keep quiet – and not play music or bring friends round. They may not be able to use scented toiletries as their brother or sister may be extremely sensitive to smells. If a parent has ME/CFS, the rest of the family may have to help more with household tasks, and may have to become carers themselves. Parents and partners often have to give up jobs in order to care for the ill person.

ME/CFS Affects Us All

Anstice

A small pointed face among the plump swathes
Of duvet and blanket, is all one can see
Of my sister, as she steadfastly braves
The draining and featureless land of ME

Like a fog or a blackout it smothers the whole
Of Anstice's energy, spreading a twilight
That dims all the channels and strangles the soul
Leaving one tiny flame, that is less than a pilot

From which she must summon the force that she needs
For the absolute minimum daily essentials.
Can't hold her eyes open, and therefore can't read:
Can't draw and can't write, as she can't hold a pencil.

Beneath the sheets she grows slender and long
Like a Michaelmas daisy; reared without sunlight,
Whose pale stem is not sufficiently strong
To bear the beautiful petalled head upright.

But, dormant beneath the thick silt of fatigue,
A spark yet remains, that no illness can hide;
Awaiting rekindling it patiently breathes
And the soul and the laughter are still in her eyes.

Rosemary Johnson

ME for Me

My mum has ME
(She is stuck in bed).
And dad is at work,
Me and my brother
Have to do all the work

Ellen Stone, age 10 ½

There Was an Old Lady...

There was an old lady with ME
Who should have been fit as a flea
Her life with Chronic Fatigue
Meant she was out of her league
When it came to lifelong energy.

Ian Stone, age 46 ¹¹/₁₂

Life is Always Tiring

Life is always tiring,
Especially when you're walking on copper wiring,
But when you're house-bound with a dog,
You'll always find yourself nice and snug,
You are falling asleep.

Will Stone, age 11

For Buddy the Dog

My mum has ME,
But she still plays with me
Takes me for walks,
Gives me food and washing-up to do
There are fun times and sleepy times,
Late mornings and late nights
(Sometimes snoozes in between)
My mum has ME
But she's up and about each day,
When I die or she dies,
I will always remember
My mum has ME.

Ellen Stone, age 10 ½

My Mum's Friend

My Mum's friend is extra-sensitive.
Mum says she has 'ME'
But I don't know what that means.
She has to stay in bed mostly.
She doesn't look poorly at all to me
But that doesn't mean she isn't though.
She lives in a bungalow so she doesn't need to move around a lot.
She has carers to look after her and help her be happy.
I feel sorry for her that she has to stay in bed in the dark.
She must be very lonely, bored and frustrated.
What a good job she has lots of friends including us.

Nina Joy Gardiner, age 6

Thank You to All Those Who Care for Us

Many people with ME/CFS are totally or partially reliant on their partners, carers and families. Without them, we could not have written this book. The poem 'To John' eloquently expresses what so many people with ME/CFS would like to say to their carers.

Thank You to All Those Who Care for Us

To John

Always patient, always caring.
Always with me to face my fears,
all my anger and all my tears.

How can I thank you, how can I say
how simply your presence, day after day,
stops me from falling into the abyss.
Helps me to realise just what I would miss?

Helping me see that a future is there,
to stop looking back and feeling despair.
To stop mourning the loss of the life that I had.
To value the good things, forget all the bad.

Yes, I do have those bleak days, those days of despair,
but I'm warm in the knowledge that you are still there.
Still waiting to catch me if I should slide,
when I want to cease swimming against that strong tide.

'Look to the horizon' you always say
'Just look to tomorrow, make the best of today'.

But I just want to thank you for all that you've done,
by helping me see that ME hasn't won.

Yes, ME will always stand in my way,
but with you there beside me,
I treasure each day.

Jo Porter

What is ME/CFS?

ME (Myalgic Encephalomyelitis) is classified by the World Health Organisation as a serious neurological illness. It is also referred to as CFS (Chronic Fatigue Syndrome) – although this also includes people who have less severe forms of fatiguing illness – or the combined ME/CFS.

ME/CFS is a disabling, long-term illness that affects an estimated 250,000 adults and children in Britain and 2,600 in Oxfordshire (i.e. 4 per 1,000, which is twice the prevalence of MS). 75% of working-age patients lose their jobs, and it can jeopardise families and friendships, causing isolation.

ME/CFS can vary widely in its severity and in the range of symptoms. It is estimated that 25% of people with ME/CFS come into the severely-affected category – meaning house-bound, wheelchair-bound or bed-bound – at some stage in their illness. Most research on treatments for the illness includes only those well enough to access hospital services. In much of the UK, those most ill are least able to access treatment.

The most common symptom of this illness is post-exertional malaise – a profound, persistent and debilitating fatigue, often made disproportionately worse by minor activity.

99

Other symptoms can include muscle, joint and nerve pain, headache, dizziness, digestive disorders, memory and concentration problems, sensitivity to light, sound and smell. It affects people to varying degrees, irrespective of lifestyle, age or gender.

Children also get ME/CFS – estimates vary as to how many, but it is at least 2 per 1000. One recent study has suggested that as many as 1% of children suffer from it, but many of these may be undiagnosed. They, and their families, have a particularly difficult time, with over half of them becoming bedridden at some stage. They may not be believed and often find it difficult to communicate how they are feeling. Their normal educational and social development is restricted by the illness. Nationally ME/CFS is the single biggest cause of long-term sickness absence from school in both children and adults.

For more information about ME/CFS, including art works illustrating the theme 'What Is ME?', please visit our website: www.oxnet.org/omega.

Oxfordshire ME Group for Action (OMEGA)

OMEGA is the support and campaign group for people with ME/CFS in Oxfordshire, UK. It is a volunteer-run group for people with ME (Myalgic Encephalomyelitis), CFS (Chronic Fatigue Syndrome), FM (Fibromyalgia) and PVFS (Post-Viral Fatigue Syndrome). We also welcome friends, families and carers.

OMEGA raises awareness about ME/CFS through various means, including an art competition and exhibition in 2010, and the poetry events in 2012 which led to the publication of this book.

OMEGA has meetings and socials throughout Oxfordshire. We have special interest groups, including a meditation group. There are regular newsletters, an optional telephone contact service, a website and an active Facebook page.

We research the needs and experiences of patients, and of doctors regarding care and treatment of ME/CFS. We successfully campaigned for a community-based service for people with ME/CFS and we continue to campaign for better treatment for sufferers, particularly children. We represent Oxfordshire ME/CFS patients and liaise with the NHS services.

FIND OUT MORE... JOIN... DONATE... VOLUNTEER...

enquire.omega@gmail.com
OMEGA 4 Bursill Close, Oxford, OX3 8EW
www.oxnet.org.uk/omega
Facebook: Search for Oxfordshire ME Group for Action
Twitter: @omega_oxon

101

Lightning Source UK Ltd.
Milton Keynes UK
UKOW040303071212

203272UK00001B/7/P